OLD WORLD INSPIRATION
FOR
AMERICAN ARCHITECTURE

PHOTOGRAPHS & TEXT
BY
RICHARD S. REQUA, A.I.A.

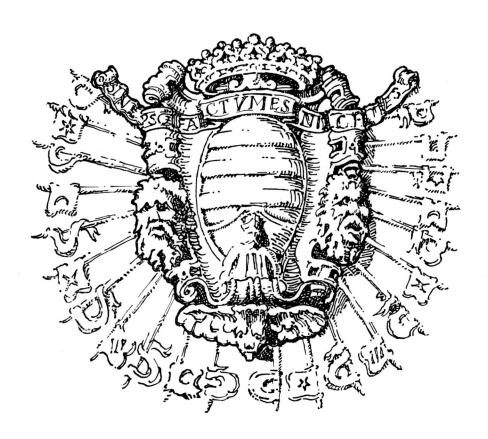

4880 Lower Valley Road, Atglen, PA 19310 USA

*To the companions
of my recent Old World travels, whose
enthusiastic interest and coöperation
inspired my best endeavors and added
so materially to the success of the trip,
this work is lovingly
dedicated*

Copyright © 2007 by Schiffer Publishing, Ltd.
Originally published by the Monolith Portland
Cement Company. Los Angeles, California.
1929
Library of Congress Control Number:
2006934729

ISBN: 978-0-7643-2668-4
Printed in China

Published by Schiffer Publishing Ltd.
4880 Lower Valley Road
Atglen, PA 19310
Phone: (610) 593-1777; Fax: (610) 593-2002
E-mail: Info@schifferbooks.com

For the largest selection of fine reference
books on this and related subjects, please visit
our web site at **www.schifferbooks.com**
We are always looking for people to write
books on new and related subjects. If you
have an idea for a book please contact us at
the above address.

This book may be purchased
from the publisher.
Include $3.95 for shipping.
Please try your bookstore first.
You may write for a free catalog.

In Europe, Schiffer books are distributed by
Bushwood Books
6 Marksbury Ave.
Kew Gardens
Surrey TW9 4JF England
Phone: 44 (0) 20 8392-8585; Fax: 44 (0) 20
8392-9876
E-mail: info@bushwoodbooks.co.uk
Free postage in the U.K., Europe;
air mail at cost.

FOREWORD

THE greatest obstacle in the path of architectural progress in America is the prevailing notion that a building of architectural pretension must be designed in some recognized ancient and exotic style.

It is the established custom to decide the question of exterior design even before the plan and practical requirements of the building are given serious consideration. Some preferred style is arbitrarily selected with little, if any, regard for fitness or congruity. Then follows the painful operation of distorting the plan and subordinating the purposes of the structure to the correctness of its external treatment. The result is a forced and more or less impracticable interior dressed in an inappropriate, academic exterior dictated by the rules and dimensions of the designer's ritual. Seldom is such a building in harmony with its environment or a true expression of its materials and purposes. Its alien ancestry is offensively obvious. Lack of inspiration and ingenuity results in banal, spiritless imitation without character or reason.

Architecture can be tersely defined as, "the science of planning, and the art of designing structures." Primarily, architecture is a science, a problem of engineering and mathematics. A building cannot approach perfection, either from the standpoint of utility or art, if the plan and structural requirements are made subservient to its design and decorative treatment. Secondarily, architecture is an art, but it cannot be classed with the fine arts if it is fettered with dogmas and formulas, nor if its products fail to satisfy the functional demands. Esthetic art recognizes no limitations, is bound by no strict rules of procedure, will not be debased by imitations or copy work. A notable work of architecture must be a creative conception skillfully executed; it must be a logical development of the plan sincerely expressing its purposes; and it must evidence in its design an honest use of the construction materials. A fundamental principle of art is harmony, and it is equally an essential in architecture. There must be harmony between plan and design, between design and environment, between beauty and utility.

Old world architecture is praiseworthy in so far as it fulfills the foregoing conditions. It is invariably the early productions, designed during the creative period, that are conceded to be the best examples of a style and the finest expressions of esthetic art. They are simple and sincere, free from pretense and shams. Inspiration and ideas were often received from the styles of other countries, frequently foreign details and construction methods were appropriated, but never was a national style wantonly plagiarized. The Spaniards, for instance, borrowed freely from their neighbors the essential ideas of their architecture, but we must go far back, almost to Egypt, to find a people who have as emphatically and persistently affirmed themselves in building.

My main purpose in the preparation of this work was to provide worthy examples of old world architecture that will stimulate the development of appropriate styles in America. For this reason I have intentionally omitted works of a monumental nature, or those concocted during the florid, decadent period of a style. I devoted my efforts rather, during my recent foreign travels, to searching out in each country visited, the simple, even primitive structures which best exemplify the character of its people and contain the vital elements of their architectural conceptions. I have further endeavored to select only photographs for this work that will furnish ideas and details of practical use in present day American architecture in the localities where favorable conditions for their utilization prevail. It is hoped, however, that they will stimulate imagination and suggest ideas appropriate to modern design rather than encourage mere imitative work. For this reason I have given no dimensions nor included measured drawings in this collection.

Not until we initiate instead of imitate, and set our minds and energies to the task of originating suitable styles for our country, can we hope for real architecture in America, architecture that will persist unaffected by transient fads and fancies, architecture that will fulfill its purposes and justify its use.

As in my previous work, "Architectural Details, Spain and the Mediterranean", I have classified the photographs and arranged the details for their most advantageous use by the architectural profession, for whom this book was especially prepared.

RICHARD S. REQUA.

LIST OF PLATES

SECTION A—STREET SCENES AND GENERAL VIEWS

SECTION B—BUILDINGS—COUNTRY TYPE

SECTION C—BUILDINGS—CITY TYPE

SECTION G—BALCONIES

SECTION H—COURTS AND PATIOS

SECTION I—GARDEN DETAILS

SECTION J—STAIRWAYS—CEILINGS—FIREPLACES

SECTION K—FOUNTAINS, FLOORS, WALLS AND GATES

SECTION L—ORNAMENTAL IRON WORK

SECTION A
STREET SCENES AND GENERAL VIEWS

STREET SCENES AND GENERAL VIEWS

THE general characteristics of an architectural style are determined: first, by environment; second, by construction materials available; third, by regional tastes and peculiarities.

As steep roofs are non-essential in arid countries, and log cabins are out of place in localities devoid of trees, so are the orders of ancient Greece incongruous in modern America. Of the few real architectural styles developed in our country, two deserve special mention. They are: the Indian pueblos of Arizona, and the colonial buildings in California. These are notable and praiseworthy in spite of the fact that they conform to no recognized canons of style. They may be primitive and lacking in cultural refinements, yet they can be classed as real architecture because they belong to the localities in which they were erected and express so completely the character and individuality of their builders. The merit of an architectural design cannot be determined by its excellence per se; it must always be studied and judged in relation to its epoch and environment.

The photographs for this section were selected particularly to emphasize these important considerations in building design, congenial relationship between buildings and their surrounding influences.

Street Scene in Rabat, Morocco.

This primitive arcade contains elements, particularly in the columns, later developed to such exquisite grace and perfection by the Moors in Spain. Arches of semi-circular shape and so simple in treatment are unusual in North Africa.

Plate 1.

A Vista of Ronda, Spain, through the
old Roman Bridge Arch.

A characteristic village scene in Andalusia. Narrow,
meandering streets lead up the hillside through the
cluster of simple, low buildings with whitewashed stuccoed walls and sagging tile roofs. Fronting an open
square, or plaza, in the center of the town rises the church
or cathedral, whose ornamented tower dominates the
picturesque scene.

Plate 2

Plate 3

The Village Well.

An interesting scene on the main road between Seville and Huelva, Spain. The water for domestic purposes in the small towns and many of the cities is supplied from fountains and wells located along the highways or in the plazas. These watering places are the scene of greatest activity in the small communities from early morning until late at night. It is the favorite gossiping place for the women and playground for the children.

Plate 3

Along the Miel, Algeciras, Spain.

The Miel is a small stream flowing into the bay of Algeciras and forming the harbor of the town. Along its banks are picturesque Andalusian cottages reminiscent of the long occupation of the town by the Moors. Luxuriant semi-tropical foliage enhances the beauty of the scene.

Plate 4

A hillside Street in Algeciras.

An interesting treatment of a stairway leading from the harbor road to the narrow, hillside streets of this quaint old town across the bay from Gibraltar. This settlement was founded by the Moors in 713, two years after their first invasion of Spain.

Plate 5

The Church of Santa Maria la Mayor,
Ronda, Spain.

Near the center of the old town, and facing a delightful little plaza, rises this beautiful tower of the church, originally a Moorish mosque. It is a most interesting architectural composition with the two-storied gallery flanking the tower on the right.

Plate 6

A Characteristic Street Scene in Palma, Mallorca.

The architecture of this charming metropolis of the Balearic Isles is awe-inspiring in its massiveness. The building facades along the narrow streets are veritable fortresses in appearance. The effect of mystery and gloom is further enhanced by wide overhanging cornices, heavy projecting balconies and ponderous stone arches.

Plate 7

Corner of Cathedral Square, Cadiz, Spain.

A delightful composition illustrating Spanish ingenuity in the use of simple elements in architectural design. Plain wall surfaces relieved with arches, window grilles, balconies and flowering plants are characteristic of their style.

Street Scene in Cadiz, Spain.

In order to give their churches and important public buildings due prominence and proper perspective, they are faced on large, open squares or located at the end of streets. The double hipped roof on the church shown is ingeniously picturesque and typical of Spanish disregard of conventionality.

Plate 8

A Street Leading from the Plaza
in Illescas, Spain.

Another delightful example of plain, simple buildings
dominated by a beautiful church tower ingeniously
placed at an angle in the street.

A Street Scene in Ecija, Spain.

The severe simplicity of the light stuccoed buildings
along the narrow streets contrasted with the brilliant
polychrome tiled church towers makes a composition
strikingly beautiful.

Plate 9

A Street in the Albaicin, Granada, Spain.

The Albaicin is northernmost of long stretched hills upon which the original city of Granada was built. It was formerly the home of the Moorish aristocracy. Along its narrow, rambling streets are to be found some of the finest examples of the old Moorish houses in Southern Spain.

The Main Street in a Village on the Highway between Madrid and Toledo.

The naive simplicity of the minor architecture and country buildings is a never-ending delight to the artist and beauty lover in Spain. That architectural beauty is not dependent upon elaboration or ornamentation has been convincingly demonstrated by the Spaniards.

Plate 10

A Picturesque Street Corner in Cordova.

In this former metropolis of Moorish Spain, the maze of narrow streets reveal enchanting vistas and new delights at every turn. Here is seen another pleasing composition of the simple elements of Spanish architecture.

A Characteristic Street in Old Cordova.

In spite of departed greatness and christian vandalism, Cordova is still the most Moorish of Spanish cities. Its architecture is a true expression of the native art of the people.

Plate 11

An Old House in Segovia.

Segovia is one of the most venerable and neglected cities in Castile. It is a veritable museum of Romanesque churches and medieval palaces. In this city of the past are to be found many picturesque old buildings suggesting ideas for modern work.

The Old Roman Bridge (El Puente),
Segovia, Spain.

This view of the largest and most remarkable piece of old Roman work now extant in Spain, was taken at its highest point where it crosses the main road in the lower town. Built in the time of Augustus, the entire structure, 2700 ft. long and consisting of 119 arches varying in height from 23 ft. to 94 ft., is formed of granite blocks set without mortar or fastenings of any kind. Much of the original work remains in perfect condition, and the aqueduct still supplies the city with water.

Plate 12

SECTION B
BUILDINGS—COUNTRY TYPE

BUILDINGS—COUNTRY TYPE

THE architecture of a nation is usually judged by its spectacular building achievements, its awe-inspiring temples or cathedrals, its imposing public edifices and its grandiose palaces. Except in rare instances, such monumental works have been the consummate ambition of rulers and leaders in wealth and influence. Often they are displays of pomp and pretense quite foreign to popular character and ideals.

The representative architecture of a people is to be found in the minor buildings and, particularly, in their country houses. Beyond the confines of the city, the native predilection and art instinct could be expressed unhampered by urban restrictions. There was little incentive in the freedom of the open spaces to be superficial or to strive for vainglorious effects. Practical problems were paramount and, usually, local materials only were available for construction purposes. These considerations, together with the natural features of the site, determined the general character and treatment of the buildings.

The rural buildings and country houses, therefore, usually express the popular tastes and preferences and, to a high degree, the fundamental principles of good architecture.

House near Cattaro, Jugo-Slavia.

A harmonious element in a wildly picturesque section of the Dalmatian coast. Cattaro is an unspoiled relic of the Middle Ages, serenely hidden at the end of a long, mountain-walled bay, as narrow and tortuous as a Norway fjord.

Plate 13

Small Country House near Naples, Italy.

A charming composition of lines, arches and flat roofs suggesting interesting ideas for the treatment of buildings in semi-arid sections of America.

Hillside House near Road to Amalfi, Italy.

Delightfully simple and unconventional is the style of country houses in Italy. The pergola, arcades, outside stairway, etc., are all features of Italian country architecture, providing intimate relation between house and garden.

Plate 14

A Country House near Ronda, Spain.

On the large estates in Andalusia, the farm buildings are frequently arranged to form an extensive patio enclosed by the group similar to the one here illustrated. The entrance to the patio is a gateway sufficiently large to admit a carriage or man on horseback.

Plate 15

BUILDINGS—COUNTRY TYPE

A Hillside Cottage near Malaga, Spain.

An example of the simple little whitewashed cottages that nestle in the rich green and brilliant flora of the Andalusian countryside. Fairly gleaming in the sunlight, they add a delightful charm to the landscape of Southern Spain.

Old Building on Road between
Seville and Huelva.

Strikingly daring and unconventionally picturesque, the buildings of Spain are a revelation to the seeker of inspiration for architectural expression.

Plate 16.

Country House on Road between
Ronda and Grazalema.

A fine example of Spanish country-house architecture.
Note the delightful informality of the design and satisfying harmony with its environment.

Plate 17.

Plate 18.

Entrance to Gardener's Cottage, Alcazar Gardens, Seville.

Composed of the simplest elements, this entrance is strikingly rich and lovely. Color, especially as supplied by the rich azulejos (colored tile) is a most effective feature of Spanish design.

Corner of Patio in a Tile Factory, Granada.

The strongest appeal of Spanish architecture is its ingenuous simplicity, its freedom from affectation and pretense.

Plate 18.

Plate 19.

Hillside Villa near Granada.

On many of the country estates in Southern Spain, a view tower is a prominent feature of the design, particularly if the building occupies a commanding site.

Plate 19.

House on Road between Granada and Cordova.

When the buildings are not sufficiently extensive to form a patio, many of the country houses of Spain have areas adjoining the building enclosed with high masonry walls. These courtyards are entered from the outside through quaint gateways as here shown.

Old Building near Tarragona, Spain.

Even the crudest of antiquated buildings in Spain will ofttimes contain ingenious structural features of unusual charm.

Plate 20.

Villa La Granja near Palma, Mallorca.

Tucked away in wooded glens on the beautiful island of Mallorca (the largest of the Balearic Isles) are many country villas of patrician size and adornment. While savoring of the Italian Renaissance, the ornamentation of these fine old buildings is sufficiently restrained to maintain harmonious relations with their picturesque environment. Following Spanish precedent, the buildings surround spacious patios which usually feature a fountain and a stairway leading to the family apartments on the second floor. In order to admit sufficient sunlight and air to the patio, the side facing the south was either built lower than the other enclosures or finished with an open arcade, serving as a covered passage connecting the side wings, as here shown. Contrary to Spanish practice, the exterior plaster of Mallorcan houses is tinted in soft pastel shades, usually light buff, enlivened with bands and borders of strong color.

Plate 21.

A wayside shop near Moguer, Spain.

These diminutive roadside buildings of Southern Spain are often delightful bits of simple architectural design.

Cottage in Establiments, Mallorca.

The unusual surface treatment of the ivory toned stucco on this little house is a quaint conceit seen only in the vicinity of Establiments.

Modern Country House near London, England.

An unusually fine example of a modern English rural home designed in the spirit of the traditional style of the country. The friendly relation between the house and its setting is quite apparent in the photograph.

Plate 23.

Two English Rural Houses.

Stone, brick, timber and stucco were the local materials combined in the construction of the quaint old houses of England. These buildings rely on simple, bold lines, good proportions and soft, warm colorings instead of surface ornament for architectural excellence. The cottages here illustrated are indeed a part of their colorful rural environment.

Plate 24.

SECTION C
BUILDINGS—CITY TYPE

BUILDINGS—CITY TYPE

THE cities of the old world and even the smaller communities were very constricted in area and compactly built. This is particularly true in the historic countries surrounding the Mediterranean. In the midst of the settlement, and usually on a prominence facing an open square, towered the principal religious edifice, mosque, temple or cathedral. From a distance, these aspiring structures call to mind huge birds hovering over a flock of fledglings. The buildings of the community cluster around the base of these exalted sanctuaries, seeming to vie and struggle for a favored position under their protecting walls. Within definitely limited confines the city is congested. Beyond its walls there are no scattering suburbs, no easy gradation from community to country. Reluctantly even have the buildings given way for streets or means of intercourse. Aimlessly the roads and passages seem to wander, twisting, turning, faltering as they thread their uncertain way through the congestion of buildings. Frequently they narrow to a single trackway barely wide enough to pass the ubiquitous burro. Unexpectedly, and without apparent reason, they may suddenly terminate in a cul-de-sac.

Under such conditions there was little opportunity for architectural display. Fortunately, the buildings are low, seldom over two stories in height. Aside from the roofs, the only portions visible are the facades fronting the narrow streets. Ambitious and ornate architectural endeavors would have been ineffectual due to lack of distance for necessary perspective. Happily, the people were endowed with art propensities, and intuitively sensed good values and proportions. Their builders were but artisans yet they made the most of the crude materials with which they worked. Therefore, from necessity as well as from choice the minor and domestic architecture of the old world cities was simple and often severe. But it is this honest, naive simplicity that gives those interesting old buildings their real charm and merit. Without trained technic or skilled craftsmanship, they produced real architecture by virtue of constructive ingenuity and natural resourcefulness.

As a rule, the wall surfaces were left severely plain, and their artistic impulses given vent in the treatment of roofs and cornices, adornment of doorways, fashioning of window grilles and balconies, and the embellishment of exquisite garden courts and patios. The fine art expressed in the execution of these structural features is worthy of serious study for much can be gained in inspiration as well as emulation, for the betterment of architecture in America.

Governor-general's Residence, Rabat, Morocco.

A modern building designed in the spirit of the simple, Arabic architecture of the Barbary Coast. A pleasing composition of plain whitewashed walls, flat roofs, balconies and tile hooded window bays. The severity of the design is further relieved by the rich foliage of the surrounding gardens.

Plate 25.

BUILDINGS—CITY TYPE.

Buildings on a Main Thoroughfare in Tunis.

An interesting feature of the buildings on the south Mediterranean coast are the window and door hoods, used to protect the openings from the intensity of the tropical sun.

Characteristic of the Moorish work so elaborately developed in Spain, the doors are often masterpieces of craftsmanship. Sometimes they are intricately paneled but more often in Tunis they are built up of vertical slabs richly studded in Arabic designs.

Plate 26.

BUILDINGS—CITY TYPE.

Plate 27.

A Characteristic Building Group in Old Algiers.

A picturesque composition of flat roof buildings near
the Kasbah and upper entrance to the old Moorish town.
With innate artistry, the Arabian colonists have piled
their cube-like structures up the steep hillsides and relieved monotony with delightful touches of strong color.
Frescoes and bright colored tile are usually employed for
this purpose.

Plate 27.

BUILDINGS—CITY TYPE.

An Old Building in Monreale, Sicily.

Excepting a few monumental structures, the building art of Sicily is quite elementary. Yet an engaging beauty has been secured in even the humblest dwellings by interesting proportions and pleasing development of practical details.

A Suburban Building near Naples.

Typical of southern Italy, even in the town buildings generous spaces are provided where possible, for outdoor living—terraces, balconies, loggias, etc., connecting with the living rooms.

Plate 28.

BUILDINGS—CITY TYPE.

A Group of Buildings in Funchal, Madeira.

No one knew better than the dwellers near the Mediterranean how to obtain pleasing effects with roofs and the simplest of architectural elements. Cobalt blue and tawny yellow were often used as a base color, and around windows and doors with striking effect.

Old Moorish Building in the Albaicin, Granada.

Limited to rough stone for walls, burned clay for roofs, whitewash for finish and wrought iron for embellishments, this frugality of materials did not deter the early dwellers in sunny Spain from expressing character and simple beauty in their primitive structures.

Plate 29.

Plate 30.

Building in Alcala, Spain.

A delightful example of simple composition illustrating particularly the effective use of balconies and roof gardens made by the Spaniards. There is no fussy ornament to detract from its charm.

Plate 30.

Plate 31.

Residence near Plaza de San Fernando, Seville.

A good illustration of the characteristic architecture of Spain. Severely plain walls, ornament restricted to the treatment of the entrance. An iron-railed balcony, as here shown, is often featured as a part of the decorative scheme, resting on the architrave.

House near the Alcazar, Seville.

An example of the simpler type of Andalusian city houses. In the early days, when protection was necessary, the entrances were made large enough to admit horses and vehicles to the inner courts or patios. Third stories on dwellings were unusual in Spain but were sometimes added as an open gallery to shelter the second floor and provide storage space.

Plate 31.

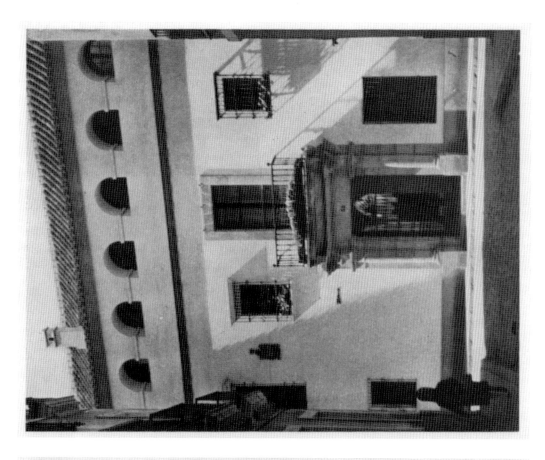

BUILDINGS—CITY TYPE.

Plate 32.

House in La Palma, Southern Spain.

A more ambitious use of ornament on domestic buildings than is usual in Andalusia. Its use here, however, is restrained and logically placed to support the lines and structural features of the building.

Entrance Facade of a palace in Seville.

The finish of this building is a conspicuous relief from the prevailing white stucco. The stone facade is executed in the typical Spanish manner with the interest focused entirely on the entrance treatment.

Plate 32.

BUILDINGS—CITY TYPE.

Plate 33.

A Government Building in Palma, Mallorca.

The buildings of Mallorca are characterized by heavy cut stone masonry construction supporting tile roofs with wide overhanging cornices. Rafter ends and projecting beams were often interestingly cut and carved. From spacious courtyards imposing stairways lead to the main rooms on the second floor.

Plate 33.

BUILDINGS—CITY TYPE.

An Apartment Building in Algeciras, Spain.

In the cities of Southern Spain many people of the working class live in apartment buildings facing or surrounding courtyards. These centers of community life are interesting both from the architectural standpoint and for the opportunity it affords to observe the real character and customs of the people.

Buildings in Grazalema, Spain.

Tucked away in the mountain fastnesses of the Sierra del Pinar, is one of the quaintest and most picturesque towns of Spain. From a distance the buildings precariously clinging to the mountainside fairly scintillate in their ever fresh dress of whitewash.

Plate 34.

The Old Church of San Juan, Segovia, Spain.

This fine old Romanesque church, now partly in ruins, is particularly interesting to visitors for the reason it now houses the ceramic studio established by the celebrated painter, Daniel Zuloaga.

Plate 35.

Plate 36.

Two Characteristic Houses in Segovia.

The unusual surface ornamentation of these buildings is a sort of crude graffito work and covers the entire facades. The designs are formed by roughly chiseling away the finish coat of stucco leaving the figures in relief against the undercoat. The design is usually a rich ivory tone and the background is gray. The effect is curious but not displeasing. This work seems to be peculiar to the vicinity of Segovia as it was not observed elsewhere.

Plate 36.

SECTION D
ROOFS—TOWERS—CORNICES—CHIMNEYS

ROOF—TOWERS—CORNICES—CHIMNEYS

IF there were no other commendable features of Old World buildings, the fine sense of proportion, scale and texture evidenced in the design and treatment of the roofs on even the least prepossessing of those venerable structures would be sufficient to class them as worthy architecture. A propensity for beauty never influenced good judgment and nothing was done simply for artistic effect. The purpose of a roof is to provide protection from the elements, and as such it was always considered and treated. Its pitch, or slope, was governed by climatic conditions rather than by fanciful ideas of the designer. Therefore, in arid countries, roofs are generally flat. Where climate is mild and rainfall moderate, a slight inclination prevails. As atmospheric conditions become more rigorous, they are consistently made steeper and sturdier. Without appearance of conscious effort, the roofs admirably suit their structures and harmonize with their environment.

The adjuncts of the roof—cornices, towers and chimneys were also treated with the same high regard for fitness. Grace and beauty were always subservient to practical requirements. These auxiliary features are meritorious because they reveal sincerity of purpose and a logical refinement of structural necessities. They evidence no struggling and straining for artistic effects.

To no small extent is the attractiveness of roofs in semitropical countries, such as surround the Mediterranean, due to the roof covering,—rounded tiles of burned clay. They were often very crudely made by hand from plastic earth found near the building sites, and moulded into form over the thigh of the workman. In addition to their insulating, weather and fire resisting properties, tile roofs possess a color blending and texture that harmonize splendidly with almost any natural setting.

Overlooking Ragusa, Jugo-Slavia, from the
old City Walls.

Venerable and antiquated, Ragusa is one of the best
preserved of medieval fortified cities. The picturesque
value of well proportioned and interestingly treated
roofs, dormers and chimneys is fully appreciated when
they are viewed from the top of the towering battle-
ments. Although limited in size to a comparatively small
city by its massive encircling walls, Ragusa was, during
the Middle Ages, one of the great harbor cities of southern Europe. From the middle of the 15th century it was
the home of a remarkable literary movement stimulated
by the Renaissance.

Plate 37.

Two Old Country Buildings near Granada.

The environs of Granada are particularly rich in fine old rambling country buildings. Apparently additions have been made to them as necessity demanded without affectation or formality. As a result the roof surfaces are delightfully varied and to this can be attributed their quaint charm.

Plate 38.

A church in the Albaicin, Granada.

This fine old church occupying a sightly position on the first settled of Granada's hills arrests the attention because of the boldness of its design and the picturesque variety of its roof lines and surfaces. Seldom does a public building as sincerely express the simple tastes of the people, without pretense or ostentatious display.

Plate 39.

A Group of Old Buildings in Algeciras, Spain.

Where but in southern Spain can be seen roofs treated with such confident boldness and at the same time such joyous abandon! After prolonged exposure to the weather, the tiles have mellowed to a rich tawny brown, toning so agreeably with the Andalusian landscape.

A Primitive Cottage in Illescas, Spain.

Even the decorative value of shadows was appreciated by the Spaniards. The ever-changing shadow lines of the roof projection on the angled whitewashed wall give unusual interest to this simple dwelling.

Plate 40.

A Picturesque Group of Old Buildings near
Ronda, Spain.

A splendid illustration of the architectural beauty of
long simple roof lines. Primitive and crude as these buildings are, they have been raised to excellence by virtue of
fine proportions and harmonious roof treatment. Note
how cleverly the fine strong lines of the roofs have been
emphasized by whitewashing the border tile.

Plate 41.

A Restored Section of the Generalife, near Granada.

This is a good example of the interesting brick cornice treatment developed by the Moors and used quite extensively in their important buildings throughout Spain. Note the unusual finish of the hip tile at the eaves.

Old Country Building near Granada.

Chimneys are featured on even the most humble cottage in Spain. Each city and contributory territory has developed its own peculiar style; and chimneys in the district usually follow the same general design. Round chimneys, such as here shown, are seldom seen except in the far north regions of the Pyrenees.

Plate 42.

A Composition of Roofs and Chimneys near Ronda.

So ingenious and unpretentious, so picturesque in composition and endless in variety, are the roof and chimney effects prevailing in southern Europe.

An Old House in Illescas, Spain.

Of particular interest in this picture is the peculiar hood effect formed by projecting the tile over the door at right angle to the run of the tile on the roof. An interesting gable end treatment found occasionally in Spain is an overhanging cornice effect up the rake of the roof formed by laying the tile on the entire gable at right angle as here shown.

Plate 43.

An Unusual Tower on a Rebuilt Section
of the Alhambra.

An ingenious design developed from the plan of an eight-pointed star. In spite of the severity of its treatment, it possesses an enduring charm because of the satisfying proportions of its wall surfaces, arched openings and tiled roof.

Plate 44.

Monastery Tower on Road Between La Palma
and Moguer, Spain.

Appealing in its grace and simple beauty, the tower
rises like a benediction from the rambling roofs of this
fine old building.

Tower on The Duke of Alba Palace, Seville.

One of the famous old palaces in Andalusia is that of
"del Duc de Alba" of which this tower is the culminating
feature. Protected by its roof is a superb example of
Moorish handicraft, one of the best preserved Mudejar
ceilings in Spain. See plate 115.

Plate 45.

A Moorish Cornice Treatment in Algiers.

This view is quite characteristic of cornice treatments on Moorish public buildings in North Africa. They were often elaborated with superimposed brick courses alternating straight run and 45 degree angle as shown on plate 42. The colors of the frieze and window border tile are white and cobalt blue.

Cornice on a Public Building in Ragusa, Jugo-Slavia.

A novel cornice design in which free use has been made of classical elements combined with Italian features. See plate 37 for a view of that interesting city.

Plate 46.

Cornice Detail on the Former Great Mosque, Cordova.

Characteristic of most oriental buildings, the exterior of this huge structure is a forbidding and fortress-like mass of masonry. This interesting stone cornice on the facade facing the Court of Ablutions, is one of its few architectural adornments.

Detail of Loggia, Spalato, Jugo-Slavia.

This unusually interesting ceiling and cornice, built by the Venetians, forms the covering of a great loggia facing the public square in this historic old city of the Dalmatian Coast in which is summarized over one thousand years of romance.

Plate 47.

A Group of Mediterranean Chimneys.

The versatility displayed in the design of chimneys in the Mediterranean countries is here illustrated. Reading from left to right, the locality of the examples are, upper row: Algeciras, Spain; Rabat, Morocco; Monreale, Sicily. Lower row: Ronda, Spain; Granada, Spain; Malaga, Spain.

Plate 48.

SECTION E
DOORWAYS

DOORWAYS

IT might almost be said that, from the time man first erected permanent buildings, the portal to his domicile has been the favorite base for expressing his artistic impulses, displaying his cultural ambitions, evidencing his affluence and indicating the degree of his hospitality. From time immemorial, the entrance has been the focal point of interest in architectural embellishment. During the Renaissance, the Spaniards, with their systematized mastery of decorative forms, and their genius for producing spectacular effects by contrasting ornamentation with broad areas of plain surfaces, developed the doorway to a state of charm and magnificence unequaled in architectural history.

While the doorways of antiquity were often richly elaborated, it was not until post Medieval times that the doors were more than rude slabs of wood built up of thick planks held together with dowels or bands. In lieu of hinges, they were usually swung on pins projecting from the top and bottom and fitting into sockets in the head and sill. It may be credited to the Moors who, with inherent craftsmanship and a penchant for decoration, developed the lowly door to an object of fine art. At first its plain surface was simply relieved with bolts and studs. Later, these were wrought into patterns or arranged to form interesting designs. Ornamented hinge straps, escutcheons, latches and knockers were next added for further enrichment. The advent of the paneled door gave their fancy further play and the opportunity was quickly seized to display their expert carpentry. Moulded panelwork of intricate pattern was designed, and to this was later added inlays, carving or repoussee work until, in their highest development, doors were objects of exquisite beauty.

Like much of the Moorish work, these richly ornamented doors are far too exotic and oriental in character to serve as models for American work. Consistent with the purpose of this book, only examples showing fundamental principles, or serving as inspiration and guidance in developing modern architecture were selected for illustrations herein.

DOORWAYS

Plate 49.

Entrance to Government Building in Rabat, Morocco.

It is a great satisfaction to note that the French government has at last learned from association and experience that the native style is the most logical and suitable to use in the development of their North African possessions. Much of the late work in Morocco has been designed in this picturesque and harmonious style. The architectural use of planting in this new work is also worthy of note.

Plate 49.

DOORWAYS

A Group of Simple North African Doorways.

Delightful charm and quaint beauty are expressed in the treatment of these humble doorways. Color, wrought iron and simple mouldings are used most effectively to relieve the monotony of plain whitewashed walls.

The first view is a garden gateway in Algiers; the other three are entrances to buildings in Tunis.

Plate 50.

DOORWAYS

Entrance to Museum Building in Algiers.

A praiseworthy example of native artistry is this unusual doorway. Characteristic of their intuitive knowledge of decorative principles, the door is treated very simply when the architrave is elaborated. Note the introduction of color by use of the tile frieze below the simple cornice.

Plate 51.

DOORWAYS

Plate 52.

Another Entrance to the Museum Buildings in Algiers.

This is another commendable example of Moorish art, charming in its simplicity. Color seems to exalt the Arab soul and he uses it boldly although with fine discretion wherever opportunity presents. A touch of it in the adornment of doorways adds a delightful and distinctive note impossible to obtain by other means. A freer and more harmonious use of color should be considered in the development of American architecture.

Plate 52.

Characteristic Doorways of the Western Mediterranean.

Although somewhat oriental in design, these doorways are especially noteworthy because they illustrate so obviously the fundamental purposes of architectural decoration,—to give grace, delicacy and beauty to structural features.

The two doorways on the left are in Tunis. The upper right is an entrance in Algiers, of which the doors are the special feature. A delightful tone effect being secured by building up the panels with a variety of woods. The lower right is a happy combination of Moorish and classical elements, and such combinations are frequently seen in Seville where this view was taken.

Plate 53.

DOORWAYS

Plate 54.

Entrance to the Royal Palace, Palermo, Sicily.

A gratifying relief from the exuberant embellishment of ecclesiastical and public buildings in Italian cities, is this dignified entrance to the Royal Palace, set in a blank wall of massive masonry. Note the grace and beauty of its simple ornamentation.

Plate 54.

DOORWAYS

A Variety of Doorways in Southern Europe.

The upper left shows particularly a novel door treatment in the entrance to a public building in Trau, Jugo-Slavia. The stiles and rails are strapped with sheet metal, and the panels are inset with framed grilles. The center panels are hinged to open as shown.

The upper right is a door to a church in Florence, Italy. The door is raised from commonplace by simple studding with round headed nails.

The door in the lower left is in Ronda, Spain, and bids for attention with its elaborate wrought iron hinge straps.

The lower right is a pair of doors in Toledo, Spain, of typical Moorish design, decorated both with panel-work and studs.

Plate 55.

DOORWAYS

Entrance to a House in Seville.

A feature of many Sevillian doorways in churches, public buildings and residences, is the hood gayly covered with blue and white tile laid in diaper pattern. The braces of the supporting brackets are of cast metal and, to the eye at least, are entirely too light to serve for other than a decorative purpose. In the cities of Andalusia, many of the entrances to residences are protected with iron grilled doors, often of very elaborate design.

Plate 56.

DOORWAYS

Two Doorways in Barcelona, Spain.

In the cities of the province of Catalonia, the old buildings are massive and even gloomy in appearance, constructed generally of dressed stone masonry. In architectural treatment, they show the influence of the neighboring countries, particularly France and Italy. Gothic, Renaissance and Moorish motifs have been recklessly yet harmoniously combined in the characteristic manner of the Spaniards.

The doorways illustrated are unpretentious yet pleasing in proportions and their simple decorative treatment.

Plate 57.

DOORWAYS

A Doorway in Toledo.

An example of intricate paneled door work with raised panel mouldings. This treatment is one of the most strikingly handsome ever devised. Note how its beauty is enhanced by placing it in an opening devoid of all ornamentation.

An Entrance in Cordova.

The design of this doorway bears a striking resemblance to the Colonial entrances of our Atlantic seaboard, —a paneled door hung in a paneled frame and surmounted with a spindled fanlight, the whole finished with white paint.

Plate 58.

DOORWAYS

Entrance to an Old Palace, Toledo.

The Moors appreciated the decorative possibilities of brick work and used it most effectively, both alone and in combination with stone and stucco work, in the construction of their important buildings. Many fine examples of their ornamental brick work are extant, particularly in Central and Northern Spain.

This fine old palace, now the residence of Anastasio De Paramo, del Conde de Toledo, is remarkably rich in Mudejar handicrafts, and it is further maintained as a museum of Spanish art. The main entrance, here illustrated, exhibits one of the early types of Moorish doors decorated very simply with wrought iron work.

Plate 59.

Two Doorways in Segovia, Spain.

Segovia hardly seems a part of Spain with its grim, almost forbidding fortress-like buildings constructed of dull granite blocks shaped from the boulders of the countryside. The prevailing architecture is quite Romanesque in character, well suited to the coarse building material and to the tastes and habits of its people. Here, as in other parts of Spain where the Moors have resided, they have left their ineffaceable impress,—decorative motifs, window grilles, balconies and ornamented stucco. See plate 36.

The heavy, lintled and arched doorways set in thick walls of scant ornament and fenestration are typical of Segovian architecture.

Plate 60.

SECTION F
WINDOW GRILLES

WINDOW GRILLES

A SUBORDINATE yet highly decorative feature of Old World architecture, particularly in the countries of the Mediterranean littoral, is the window grille. This was an especially important accessory in the regions where the Moors had impressed their oriental tastes and character upon the national art, as in Spain and the north African countries.

In the congestion of the cities where the buildings encroach upon and actually overhang the narrow streets, protection from night prowlers as well as security from invading hordes required the barring of all openings in the exterior walls of the lower floors. Although such defenses are no longer as necessary as during the Middle Ages when every man was a law unto himself which he freely administered according to his whims and prejudices, the practice of covering windows with lattice and gratings still prevails as an established custom. They still serve a very practical purpose by giving a sense of privacy and security to the obtruding buildings on the city thoroughfares. With the characteristic ingenuity and love of decoration, the Spaniards lavished affection on these window guards, elevating them from mere protecting bars to exquisite features of their architectural design. In many of the minor buildings and houses of Spain, the window grilles have been made the principal feature of ornamentation. Many interesting examples of grilles are to be seen in the old buildings of North Africa, some with the intricacy and delicacy of fine lace work.

While there are few opportunities to use them in American buildings, the Old World grilles are worthy of study as models of decorative design and skilled craftsmanship.

WINDOW GRILLES

Plate 61.

Oriental Window Treatments in Tunis.

The two most common window treatments in North Africa are the box lattice used in combination with a protecting hood; and the projecting iron grille curving to semi-circular shape over the lower half of the opening. These latter are popularly known as "harem grilles". In Mohammedan countries all windows are closely screened to protect the women who are not permitted to show their faces to others than their husbands or immediate family.

Plate 61.

WINDOW GRILLES

Plate 62.

Two Characteristic Grilles of Southern Spain.

The simple grille in the lower view is in Ronda, and is a good specimen of the simple types generally found on the older buildings. The corner bars were often twisted, and the frame work of the head and sill covered with flat tile and stuccoed as shown. Paneled shutters are often used in the semi-tropical regions in place of sash.

The upper grille is in Algeciras, and is representative of the highly developed ornamental grilles of Spain. Algeciras is noted for its wealth of beautiful iron work.

Plate 62.

Plate 63.

Two Moorish Windows in Cordova.

Cordova, being for so many centuries the seat of Moorish art and culture in Spain, is particularly rich in fine details of Moorish architecture. These two examples are characteristic examples of their window treatments.

Plate 63.

Plate 64.

Old Building in Town near Tarragona, Spain.

The magic of even simple, crude iron work in giving
interest to buildings otherwise devoid of ornament is no-
where appreciated as in Spain. There is an unassuming
charm in this plain old building due entirely to its appropriately simple iron work.

Plate 64.

Small Decorative Grilles in Barcelona.

Window grilles were used in Spain primarily for protection and are, therefore, usually lacking in delicacy and refinement. However, small grilles of light construction and serving principally a decorative purpose, are sometimes seen.

Plate 65.

WINDOW GRILLES

Window Grilles in Illescas, Spain.

Grilles of unusual form and character, observed only in Illescas and adjacent towns, between Madrid and Toledo, are here shown. In addition to being particularly decorative, they seem the most practicable for buildings that front on narrow streets. The lower section, being flush with the building, offers no obstruction to traffic; while the projecting upper section permits views up and down the street from the interior.

Plate 66.

An unusual Grille in Sitges, Spain.

A fine example of Spanish craftsmanship showing the decorative possibilities of forged iron work. Note particularly the projecting leaf design extended from the center of the volutes, with its formidable center spikes.

Plate 67.

Two ornate windows in Sitges, Spain.

Overlooking the grotesque treatment of the enframing stonework,—a whimsical modern addition,—the grilles are fine specimens of delicately wrought iron work. The most commendable feature of Spanish iron work is that, in its design and treatment, it never loses its quality as iron or appears to be an imitation of anything else. The work always possesses that crude charm of its base metal.

Plate 68.

WINDOW GRILLES

Plate 69.

Window Grille on an Exposition Building in Seville.

Contrasted with the fine old iron work of Spain is this elaborately ornate grille on a South American building in the International Exposition at Seville. While the design is not uninteresting, the work does not possess the subtle charm and artful craftsmanship found in the old native work.

Plate 69.

Plate 70.

Stone Grilles in the Mosque of Cordova.

These delicate, pierced stone grilles are strikingly effective, set in the massive walls of this huge building. They are one of the few decorative features used to relieve the monotony of its almost forbidding exterior.

Grilles of this character are appropriately finding a place in the architecture of our Pacific Coast.

Plate 70.

WINDOW GRILLES

Plate 71.

Window Shutters in Valencia, Spain.

Many of the Old World buildings are even today without glass windows. This obtains particularly in the subtropical borders of the Mediterranean. In lieu of sash, hinged wooden shutters are used and these are often splendid examples of the wood-worker's art. Where iron grilles did not cover the openings, the shutters were made heavy for protection, and frequently richly elaborated to serve as a feature of the exterior design.

Plate 71.

WINDOW GRILLES

Plate 72.

Window Shutters in the Audiencia, Valencia, Spain.

In the fine old 16th century Renaissance building, formerly the Chamber of Deputies, are to be found these interesting specimens of Spanish molded panel work. Every window in the building is closed with heavy wooden shutters, each of a different and beautiful pattern.

Plate 72.

SECTION G
BALCONIES

BALCONIES

WHILE balconies did not come into general use until the Middle Ages, their origin dates back at least to Greco-Roman times. The etymology of the word has even been traced to a Greek word meaning "to throw", hence it is presumed that balconies were originally built for purposes of defence,—a projecting platform from which missiles could be thrown upon the attacking enemy. Balconies were found on several houses in Pompeii; and their ancient use is indicated by frescoes and reliefs, and by literary descriptions.

However, it was not until the time of the Renaissance that architects began to feature them as elements of exterior design. Since that time balconies have become increasingly popular, especially in mild climates where, by their use, the windows can extend to the floor thereby admitting more light and air to the interior. In all civilized as well as oriental lands, balconies have now become favorite motifs in architectural compositions.

During their evolution, in the many countries of their adoption, balconies have been constructed of every material serviceable for building purposes,—stone, marble, concrete, brick, wood and iron, or combinations of them. From a small projecting platform resting on brackets or consoles and surrounded by a parapet or balustrade, many variations and elaborated types have been developed culminating in the extended patio galleries of Spain and the arcaded loggias of Italy, with supports rising from the ground in the form of columns and arches. In northern Europe, the structure is frequently of wood and has been made a most picturesque feature of houses and chalets. In southern Europe balconies have become an institution, and are almost a requisite on buildings over one story in height. In southern Spain, they are converted into miniature gardens for potted plants, making them the most colorful and conspicuous note in the exterior treatment.

The prevalence of the balcony, in its various forms and treatments, on Old World buildings, indicates the practical as well as ornamental value of this desirable architectural accessory; and should encourage its more general use in American architecture.

BALCONIES

A Group of Old World Balconies.

Upper left: a balcony in Valletta, Malta, showing an interesting combination of masonry platform and supporting corbels, wood posts and hood, and iron railing.

Upper right: Balcony built entirely of wood, on a tower in Trau, Jugo-Slavia. The heavy corbelled supports with carved ends are the special feature.

Lower left: A balcony common to the rural districts of southern Italy,—an iron railed platform supported on combination masonry arches and wood or stone corbels.

Lower right: An unusually effective balcony in Toulouse, France, built of brick, with brick arches resting on carved stone consoles. The hood is independently supported on carved wood brackets.

Plate 73.

BALCONIES

Plate 74.

A Corner Balcony in Seville.

A typical flower-decked balcony of Andalusia. A combination of wrought iron, colored tile and brilliant bloom, making a spectacular feature when contrasted with the plain unadorned walls of white plaster.

Plate 74.

BALCONIES

Soffit Detail of Balcony in Seville.

A feature of special interest in the delightful treatment of balconies in southern Spain, is the soffit decoration of the balcony floors. Bright colored tile of pleasing designs are laid in the frame of the platform support and greatly enhance the brilliant effect when viewed from the street below.

A Tiled Window Treatment in Cordova.

When the windows are the sole feature of exterior ornamentation, the frames of the openings as well as the soffits of the balcony platforms are often richly treated with decorated tile. Note how cleverly the interest is centered on the tile work and the floral display by the severely simple design of the balcony railing.

Plate 75.

BALCONIES

Plate 76.

Two Architectural Balconies in Southern Spain.

Balconies are frequently made a unit of the exterior design by finishing the edges of the platforms with moldings which are extended across the face of the building as belt molds. Great variations will be noted in the construction of the balcony supports. Often they are heavy, almost massive, in appearance finished with moldings and deep fascias, or by simply corbelling or curving out the wall face. In contrast to this treatment, the platforms will be characterized by extreme lightness, either with no supports or with delicately curved braces of wrought iron.

Plate 76.

BALCONIES

Balconies on an Old House in Seville.

These beautiful old specimens of the ironcrafter's art evidence the Spaniards' affection for wrought iron work. These balconies are wonderfully effective as contrasted with the plain whitewashed walls of this simple old building.

Plate 77.

BALCONIES

Two More Window Balconies in Southern Spain.

Here are contrasted plain and ornate balconies, examples of popular types in the south of Spain. In many of the small towns and villages, the balconies are often more elaborately designed than those customarily used in the cities. This may be due to local traditions but a more reasonable explanation is the fact that buildings in the country towns are usually crudely constructed and severely plain. Considerable attention is given to the balconies therefore, as they are the only enlivening feature. It is also interesting to note that there is a similarity and harmony of balcony design in each community. This, in fact is so marked that a person versed in Spanish architecture can often determine the locality of a building by noting the treatment of its balconies.

Plate 78.

BALCONIES

Balconies and Grilles on a Building in Cordova.

It is seldom that grilles are used over second story windows in Spain, particularly in combination with balconies. The building here shown is a modern residence and, as grilles are a traditional feature, they are probably here used more for ornamental than practical reasons.

A Double Window Balcony in Ronda.

A characteristically simple detail of the buildings in Ronda, one of the best preserved old Moorish towns in Spain. So completely are its people imbued with the spirit of the old work that it is difficult to distinguish the later buildings from those erected before the Spanish conquest in 1485.

Plate 79.

BALCONIES

A Covered Balcony in Seville.

It is inherent in the Spaniard to do unconventional things in practical and commonsense ways. Wood paneled exterior doors in the second story of a house can be considered with the uncommon sights. Here is one unpretentiously treated, opening onto a wood floored balcony with a projecting tiled hood, and finished agreeably with simple ironwork.

A Loggia Balcony in Cordova.

Another example of the unusual but consistently logical treatment of an iron railed balcony adding to the attractiveness of a protected gallery or loggia.

Plate 80.

BALCONIES

Two More Balconies in Cordova.

Strong Moorish influence is shown in the simple treatment of the balcony in the upper picture. In decided contrast to the bewildering ornamentation of their palaces, the domestic architecture of the Moors was singularly devoid of surface embellishments.

The delightful treatment of the balcony in the lower picture, makes it the architectural feature of the patio in the Municipal Museum. It is located on the wall opposite the main entrance and is a convincing demonstration of the effective use of color in exterior ornamentation.

Plate 81.

BALCONIES

An Ornamental Window in Cordova.

A partial view of a modern building in which a variation of the Moorish arch is used for the window framing. The balcony is a departure from the usual Spanish treatment.

A Decorative Window in Ronda.

On a plain blank wall of cut stone masonry is featured this highly ornamented window and balcony. As can be imagined, it is wonderfully effective in its plain setting.

Plate 82.

Plate 83.

Hooded Window Balconies in Seville.

The peculiar hoods sheltering the windows shown in this view is an oriental feature much used on buildings in the tropical regions of north Africa. The braces supporting the balconies are fine examples of Spanish wrought iron work.

Plate 83.

BALCONIES

Balconies in Palma, Mallorca.

Because of their situation in the Mediterranean between Italy and Spain, the people of the Balearic Islands were influenced in their architecture by the developments in both of these countries. The important buildings and houses of the wealthy were often built of stone in a style suggestive of the Renaissance. Balconies, as in Italy, were usually made an element of the design, constructed of the stonework of the walls and surrounded either with iron railings or stone balustrades. Frequently the balconies were deeply inset and treated in the typical style of the Italian loggia.

Plate 84.

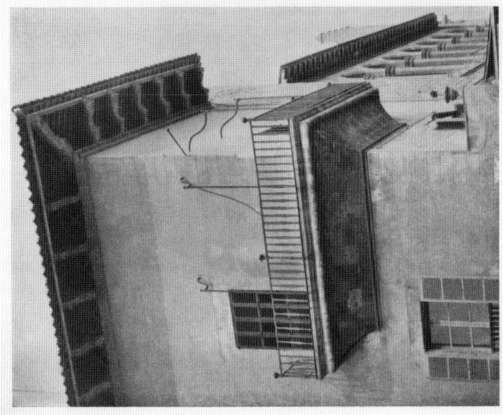

SECTION H
COURTS AND PATIOS

COURTS AND PATIOS

REGARDLESS of one's opinions concerning Mediterranean architecture, the American traveler cannot but wax enthusiastic over what is conceded to be the most delightful feature of the buildings in southern Europe, —the courts and patios. In the palace of the wealthy or the abode of the poor, they are the center, the heart of home life, around which the building is constructed.

As would be expected in the coastal regions of the Mediterranean where the climate is favorable and the rainfall slight, the inhabitants are inclined to spend as much time as possible in the open air. Places and facilities for outdoor activities are, therefore, quite essential in their daily lives. The congestion of the cities, with their dark, narrow streets, affords little opportunity for outdoor living except in such open spaces as are provided within the confines of the buildings. Consequently, the interior court becomes quite an indispensable feature of their domestic architecture. The buildings face inward on the courts instead of outward on the street. For this reason the facades are often severe and lacking in windows.

While courts are common to all warm countries of the Old World, it is in Spain that these intimate house gardens,—there called patios,—have been developed to great charm and perfection. The entrance doorway to the Spanish home, often protected by iron grille work, leads directly to the patio, from which the stairway ascends to the upper stories. The floor is paved, often with bright colored tile. Frequently, decorated tile wainscots give added brilliance to the treatment. The main feature of the patio is a quaint old well or interesting fountain around which are grouped palms, araucarias, laurels, orange trees, oleanders, ornamental shrubs and flowering plants, all in pots, except in the spacious courtyards of palaces and public buildings. Arcades or colonnades often surround the patio, sheltering the rooms from the caprices of the weather and providing a cool retreat during the heat of the long summer. The patio is freely used as an outdoor living-room, and it is here, during fair weather, that members of the family and their friends gather for social intercourse and recreation. Brightly upholstered chairs and other indoor furnishings, even including the piano, are moved out into the patio, adding domestic interest to the scene.

While courts, or patios, are hardly practicable in our American climates, nor compatible with our modern habits of living, the idea of secluded gardens connected with our homes seems worthy of serious consideration. The friendliness and inviting atmosphere of such gardens should not only encourage healthful habits of outdoor living, but add materially to the attractiveness of American homes.

An Old Moorish Courtyard in Tunis.

This simple old courtyard with its double arcade and crude decorations is an oriental feature much used in all types of buildings in north Africa. The idea was introduced into southern Europe by the Moors and developed by the Spaniards into the delightful patios of their domestic buildings.

Plate 85.

A Sumptuous Palace Court in Tunis.

The public buildings and palaces of north Africa are often architectural features of magnificence and splendor, as here illustrated. The wainscot is of richly decorated tile, Persian, as well as local motifs being used. The walls above and the arches are intricately ornamented with arabic designs impressed with molds into the soft plaster when it was applied. The rich treatment is usually carried through the galleries of the second story to the parapets of the roof.

Plate 86.

An Old Courtyard in Southern Italy.

Contrasted with the brilliance of Spanish patios, the Italian courtyards are lacking in color, but otherwise they are usually more architecturally treated. Even in the simple courts of their humble dwellings, they are often delightful in design and proportions. Arches are much used, in interesting variety, and the stairways are the prominent feature.

Plate 87.

Patio in the Municipal Museum, Cordova.

Filled with art relics of bygone centuries, and radiant with color, this forecourt to the city's famous museum is one of the most interesting attractions in Cordova. It was contrary to the religious principles of the Moors to use statuary, or any reproductions of living forms, and it is seldom seen in old Spanish gardens.

Plate 88.

An Old Moorish Patio in Cordova.

In the old section of Cordova, the Moorish impress still persists. The houses are low, decaying structures, usually one story high. Frequent coats of whitewash and trimmings of strong color keep them ever fresh and trim looking despite their age and structural dilapidation. The joy of these old houses is the patios with their riotous displays of palms, plants and bloom that never fail to call forth exclamations of surprise and delight from the visitor.

Plate 89.

Corner of a Patio in Cordova.

Another glimpse of one of the fascinating old patios in Cordova. Except for occasional arches and simple iron grilles or balconies, the vines and plants provide the only decoration. They are indeed a revelation to those seeking inspiration for true architectural expression.

Plate 90.

Plate 91.

Features of Old Andalusian Patios.

While patios are common to all of Spain wherever the Moors influenced the trend of architecture, it is in southern Spain that they become the most important and interesting features of buildings, public and private.

In the patio shown in the upper picture, multi-colored tile was sparingly used to splendid effect. The treatment of the arched opening leading to a rear passage is particularly noteworthy.

In the lower scene,—another simple old Moorish patio, —the high base of strong cobalt blue is the only relieving color from the dazzling whitewash of the walls. Orange trees in tubs and massings of small plants in terra-cotta pots add satisfying variety to the treatment.

Plate 91.

COURTS AND PATIOS

Entrance to Patio, Triana, Spain.

The quaint old town of Triana, a suburb of Seville on the opposite bank of the Guadalquivir, has from time immemorial been an important center of Spain's pottery and ceramic industry. Its factories supply most of the decorated tile—azulejos—used to enliven the walls and floors of buildings and patios in southern Spain. Wandering along its centuries old streets, the visitor, peering through the doorways to the houses, catches delightful glimpses of fine old patios.

A Diminutive Patio in Algeciras, Spain.

Regardless of size and pretension, town buildings in the south of Spain are provided with patios even if the space available is but the width of a passageway. With loving care they are kept ever trim and bright. There is always room for a cheery display of potted plants massed against, and even hung on the walls, no matter how diminutive the patio may be.

COURTS AND PATIOS

Courtyard in a Historic Old Inn, Cordova.

Among the important buildings of every Spanish town are the posadas, or inns, where the country people and native visitors find shelter, rest and food both for themselves and their animals. The vehicles, fowls and small animals are left in the courtyard while the mounts and draft animals, usually burros, are kept in stalls behind the arcade on the ground floor. Adjoining the courtyard are the dining room and primitive kitchen. The sleeping rooms are located on the second floor over the stable.

Corner of the Courtyard in the Villa La Granja, Mallorca.

While the fine old courtyards of Mallorca resemble the courts of Italy in architectural treatment, they are, nevertheless, quite Spanish in detail. This is a view of the forecourt in one of the finest country villas on the island. The real garden adjoins the building, on the right, and by reason of the slope of the ground, is on the level with the second floor, which story contains the main living rooms.

Plate 93.

Two Stable Courts, Island of Mallorca.

In connection with the villas and country houses in Mallorca it is the custom to provide an entrance or stable court in addition to the family court or patio. Often in the stable courts are to be found delightful bits of simple architectural detail, such as are shown in these views.

Plate 94.

Two Courtyards in Palma, Mallorca.

There is a sense of grandeur and massiveness in the treatment of palace courts in Mallorca that contrasts with the delicacy and airiness of the patios of Spain.

Two characteristic features of Mallorcan courtyards are the great stone arches, often spanning the entire width of the courts; and the elaborate stairways, ingeniously contrived, see plate 113, ascending to the main floor above.

Wells are often used instead of fountains as the principal note of interest. Plants are used sparingly; and the lack of strong color results in a somberness, quite at variance with the brilliance of the patios in Spain, the country of which the Balearic Islands form a province.

Plate 95.

Gallery Details in Patio of Old House in Ronda.

It is unusual in Spain to find much variation in the design of details in a building except when additions were made at later dates. The galleries here shown are in a decayed old palace in Ronda and, from the great difference noted in the treatment of the two, it is probable that the upper one was a much later addition. The gallery pictured below has the crude simplicity of the early Moorish work. Except in the colonies, the Spaniards used iron railings for balconies in preference to wooden balustrades.

The prevalence of wood grilles and spindles in the early Spanish American work was probably due to necessity rather than from choice.

Plate 96.

SECTION I
GARDEN DETAILS

GARDEN DETAILS

THE far-famed gardens of Italy are formal architectural creations, extensive in area, planned on a grand scale for spectacular effects. Usually, they were an intensive and elaborate development of kingly estates in which the residence—palace or villa—was subordinate to the landscaping project. The grounds are so expansive, and the layout so geometrically precise, that the gardens can only be comprehended when viewed from an elevation. They were designed to be overlooked rather than intimately enjoyed. The accessories are monumental and pompous in character, selected to amaze rather than to charm the beholder. Obviously these are not private gardens but public show places.

Quite the opposite in every vital particular, are the Spanish gardens and their oriental prototypes in north Africa. They are rarely of wide extent or ostentatious; and are usually enclosed as patios. Excepting some modern gardens, they are seldom symmetrical or laid out on axes. They are notably unconventional in design and treatment. While often not apparent to the casual observer, the features and accessories are placed with studied avoidance of symmetry. The primary purpose of these gardens is not to provide a grand display for the public but a pleasant retreat for the members of the household and their intimate friends. Imposing effects would obviously be incongruous in such gardens, consequently, statuary, ornate fountains and elaborate architectural appurtenances are seldom found there. Potted plants, a few choice trees, bright tiled seats, a little splash and gurgle of water, a sheltered pergola or bower; these are the unassuming adornments of the picturesque little gardens of Andalusia. Their atmosphere is that of restfulness and cheer; such an environment as should form a part of our American homes. Details and simple accessories of these unpretentious Old World gardens are illustrated in this and following sections.

A Garden Retreat in Grounds of a Hotel, Algiers.

It was an agreeable surprise to find that the new hotels, built on the heights above the native quarters and the modern city of Algiers, have been designed in a quaint style suggestive of the old Moorish work.

The most interesting features of one of the leading resort hotels is the broad, tiled terrace and the fine tropical garden it overlooks. Typical of north African gardens, there are no pretentious accessories to distract attention or mar the natural beauty of the planting.

This snug retreat not only adds a delightful oriental touch to the garden but provides a secluded place for rest and contemplation.

Plate 97.

GARDEN DETAILS

Tiled Seat on Garden Terrace, Governor's Residence, Rabat.

A novel combination of colored tile work and plants; a treatment effectively used on the new buildings erected by the French in Morocco. See plate 25 for view of this building from the opposite side.

Tiled Seat in Plaza Santa Cruz, Seville.

A modernized plaza in the heart of old Seville in which the seats in the planted borders surrounding the open promenade space, are faced with brilliantly colored tile. Colored tile is used effectively in many of the modern parks and plazas in southern Spain.

Plate 98.

GARDEN DETAILS

Garden in the Casa Del Rey Moro, Ronda.

This modern garden development is one of the principal sights in Ronda, and one of the finest small gardens in Spain. It is laid out as a series of view terraces, following approximately the slope of the hillside as it drops away towards the deep gorge, or Tajo, of the river Gaudalquivir. Contrary to Moorish precedent, the general treatment is formal although its many delightful features are quite true to Spanish tradition. Water is piped to the fountain in the center of the upper terrace, from which it is ingeniously led through open troughs in the pavement to fountains in the walls of the two lower terraces.

This device was much used in the old Moorish gardens where the conservation of water was a necessity. This view was taken from the second story terrace of the house.

Plate 99.

Garden Stairway in Villa Igea, Palermo, Sicily.

This grand stairway of Italian design leads from the Villa Igea,—Palermo's finest tourist hotel,—through the beautiful semi-tropical gardens to the rocky palisades of the wild seacoast. The feature for which the picture was taken is the use of earthernware jars as interesting garden accessories.

In a Patio Garden, Palma, Mallorca.

Situated on an elevation high above the adjacent streets, this old palace garden has an air of delightful seclusion. Except for the absence of colored tile, this garden court possesses all the charm of the simple old patios of Spain.

Plate 100.

GARDEN DETAILS

Plate 101.

Entrance to Pavilion, Murillo Gardens, Seville.

The Murillo Gardens are a long, narrow strip of parking, just beyond the east wall of the Alcazar Gardens. They are a series of small formal plots made up of flower beds, tiled fountains and seats. At the north end of the gardens is this interesting little structure, a modern building suggestive of the pavilion built for Charles V in the Gardens of the Alcazar.

Plate 101.

Seats in Wall of Alcazar Gardens, Seville.

The most delightful features of the extensive gardens of the Alcazar are the series of quaint old patios adjoining the palace. The plain, massive walls, finished with whitewashed stucco, are relieved by orange trees trained and flattened against the surface. Occasionally openings through the thick walls, faced with tile and provided with seats, form an inviting retreat from the heat and glare of the Andalusian sun.

Plate 102.

GARDEN DETAILS

Garden Entrance to a Building in Algiers.

The Moors availed themselves of every opportunity to use potted plants in their gardens. Even the stair parapets were formed in steps to provide places for pots. Aloes, with their flaming red bloom are strikingly effective against the white walls of the building, used as a stairway decoration in this building.

Stairway in Generalife Gardens, Granada.

Here again, in the famous gardens of the Generalife, are the parapets of the stairway constructed in the customary manner of the Moors for the purpose of displaying potted plants.

Plate 103.

GARDEN DETAILS

Looking Down upon the Walls in the Gardens
of the Generalife.

Another illustration of the effective use of plants in pots in the gardens of southern Spain. While requiring constant care, they add greatly to the interest of garden walls, especially when viewed from above.

Small Building in a Palace Garden, Cordova.

To one seeking delightful bits of simple Moorish architecture, this little shelter used as a gardeners' workshop, is the most interesting feature in the palace gardens of the Marquis de Viana. Wall pots, as shown here, filled with flowering plants, are extensively used for decorating the plain walls of the patios in southern Spain.

Plate 104.

GARDEN DETAILS

An Interesting Curb Treatment in a Park, Seville.

An ingenious way to terminate a curb at a road inter-section, is here shown. It is frequently used in the parks of Seville, with a palm planted in the circle formed by the return of the curb. As will be noted, even the street curbs are edged with tile, usually alternating blue and white.

Ornamental Jars in a Patio, Cordova.

In place of statuary or other useless accessories, the Spaniards obtain variety in their gardens and patios by using large ornamental jars as receptacles for potted plants.

Plate 105.

GARDEN DETAILS

Ornamental Jars and Plant Holders in Patios,
Southern Spain.

Decorated flower pots and quaint terra cotta jars set
in wrought iron stands are cherished features of Spanish
gardens and patios. The single pot illustrated graces the
corner of a garden in Cordova. The group of unusual jars
is in a patio in Seville.

Plate 106.

Tile Covered Plant Boxes in Spanish Patios.

For trees and large shrubs, the containers are often made of cement and finished with decorated colored tile to harmonize with the treatment of wainscots and floors.

The lower view was taken in a patio in Cadiz. The upper scene is in a small house patio in Illescas.

Plate 107.

Plate 108.

Examples of Large Jars Featured in the Gardens
of Spain.

The decorative qualities of earthenware jars combined
with wrought iron, also their appropriateness as interesting garden accessories, are fully appreciated by the
Spaniards. The jars, as here illustrated are to be found
in patios and gardens of Algeciras, Seville, Cordova and
Toledo.

Plate 108.

SECTION J
STAIRWAYS—CEILINGS—FIREPLACES

STAIRWAYS—CEILINGS—FIREPLACES

WHILE stairways, or some arrangement of steps or inclines, have always been necessary for communication between floors in structures of more than one story in height, it was not until the Middle Ages that they were treated with any importance in the design of buildings. They were first given a position of prominence and dignity in the palaces of Italy during the Renaissance. With the increasing popularity of multi-storied buildings, stairways soon came to the fore as one of the most interesting and ornate features of interior design. In the regions of favorable climate adjacent to the Mediterranean, they were frequently placed on the exterior, rising gracefully from the courts and patios to the floors above. Great skill has been displayed in the design and construction of these important accessories; the steps have often been ingeniously carried on wide spanning rampant arches, built entirely of brick or stone masonry. They are one of the most picturesque features of Old World buildings.

Except in the churches, public buildings and palaces of Spain, the interior walls of old buildings are quite barren of architectural interest. Strangely, the buildings were planned with no special regard for the use or fitness of the rooms. The only distinguishing characteristic is the ceilings; and it was on the treatment of these that the skill of both architect and artisan was concentrated. During the centuries of architectural contriving in Spain, almost every type of ceiling used in neighboring countries was adapted to their buildings. For general consideration, they may be divided into three classes: the geometrical, stalactite development of Mohammedan art, executed in plaster; the various framed types in which the beams, rafters and other construction members were left exposed; and the richly ornamented coffered ceilings of the Renaissance. The Mohammedan ceilings find no place in modern architecture, therefore, no examples of this style are shown. Wood ceilings, in their many variations were freely used in Spain, from crude horizontal beams supporting level ceilings of plain plaster, to the most intricate designs in exposed rafter and truss work. The execution of these latter ceilings, in the buildings erected by the Spaniards following the conquest, was by those master craftsmen the Moors and is known as Mudejar work. With the advent of the Renaissance, the art lost much of its fine character, and the design was often reduced to a horizontal cross-beaming below a flat ceiling, forming coffers. The construction members were covered and lavishly ornamented in the conventional styles of the period.

Fireplaces have not occupied the conspicuous place in Spanish buildings that they have in Italy and other European countries. Usually they were built in projections of the walls to provide sufficient depth for the fire, and were strictly utilitarian features. However, like much of the simple architectural work of Spain, they are interesting because of pleasing proportions and ingenious design. The two fireplaces illustrated are not typical but interesting examples of the few ornamental old fireplaces in Spain.

Typical Stairways in Houses of Spain.

The grace and picturesque beauty of Spanish stairways can be appreciated from the characteristic treatments shown in these pictures. The structural as well as the decorative possibilities of arches are fully realized by the Spaniards. Seville (lower) and Palma (upper) furnished the subjects for these illustrations.

Plate 109.

Mediterranean Examples of Outside Stairways.

The upper picture was taken near Amalfi and illustrates the type of stairways generally used on the exterior of country buildings in southern Italy. They lead directly from streets or open gardens instead of from courts as in Spain.

The lower picture is a specimen of the simple stairways often seen in the old courtyards of large buildings on the Island of Mallorca.

Plate 110.

Two Imposing Stone Stairways in Spain.

The architectural developments on the east coast of Spain were strongly influenced by the Gothic and Renaissance work of the neighboring countries, France and Italy. The buildings, of dull gray stone, are rather grim and massive in appearance relieved somewhat by the lavish use of carved stone ornament. Prepossessing stairways with richly carved parapets tend to relieve the oppression of the somber courtyards.

Plate 111.

Stairway in Municipal Building, Trau, Jugo-Slavia.

Trau is a picturesque little island village on the wild and rugged coast of Dalmatia; the scene of conquering conflicts with Hungarians, Turks and Venetians. It is particularly interesting for its remains of Venetian domination although the Saracens left an oriental impress in its narrow, shadowed streets. Forming one side of its public square is the stately municipal building in which the stairway illustrated graces the stern architecture of its courtyard.

Plate 112.

An Elaborate Stairway in Palma, Mallorca.

The Mallorcans delight in the use of the arch and employ it boldly and skillfully as important supporting members in the construction of their courts and stairways. The second story of their buildings frequently overhangs portions of the courtyard, and is supported on great stone arches.

These arches are carried in a wide span across the courtyard, resting on short, thick columns at their intersections. The stairways are a dignified, almost monumental feature, often carried on an ingenious arrangement of arches and columns, as here shown.

Plate 113.

Ceiling in Alcazar, Seville.

The Alcazar has been a royal residence ever since the city was wrested from the Moors in 1248. The palace was rebuilt during the following century and the work was done by Moorish artisans in the voluptuous, oriental style of the Alhambra. The artesonado ceilings, intricately designed in geometrical, Moresque patterns, were particularly fine examples of their craftsmanship. Unfortunately, these wooden ceilings were almost wholly destroyed by the fire of 1762 and it was after the middle of the following century before they were rebuilt. In the reconstruction, little consideration was given to archeological accuracy, but several of them were restored to approximately their original form and coloring.

The octagonal ceiling here shown is typical of the fine skill displayed in design and workmanship.

Plate 114.

Ceiling in the Duke of Alba Palace, Seville.

One of the finest Mudejar ceilings in Spain is this beautiful artesonado in the room under the tower roof illustrated on plate 45. It was brought to light only a few years ago when a plaster sub-ceiling was removed during alterations in the palace. It was in such perfect condition that only a touching up of the color work was required.

Mudejar Ceiling in the Santa Cruz Hospital, Toledo.

This is the center section of a ceiling, between the tie beams, that covers one of the long second-story dormitories. It is in the natural wood without color decoration. The lower face of the tie beams is finely carved, as shown. The center pendant is overlaid with gold in the customary manner.

Plate 115.

Two Wooden Ceilings of Moorish Design
in Toledo.

Toledo is not only the most venerable city in Spain, but is considered the oldest city in Europe. Established centuries before the Christian era, it was a thriving city in 193 B. C. when occupied by the Romans. It was later captured in turn by the Goths and Moors. Although it was wrested from the infidels in 1085, it still contains many evidences of Moorish occupation. For centuries after, the architecture of Toledo was strongly influenced by the art and skill of the Moors which is evidenced by the fine Mudejar ceilings in the important buildings of the city, erected as late as the 16th century.

Plate 116.

A Wood Coffered Ceiling in Toledo.

This is a fine example of the Spanish treatment of wood coffered ceilings. The coffers are formed with deep wood moldings, and the soffits are wood panels carved in relief. The entire ceiling is finished in the deep rich brown tone of aged wood.

A Flat Wood Ceiling in Seville.

This ceiling, in an arcade facing a patio in the Duke of Alba's palace, is unusually simple and effective. It was constructed, first by nailing wide boards, tight jointed, directly on the bottom of the ceiling joists. Then the moldings were nailed to the boards to form the hexagonal panels.

The color scheme was simple but effective, being done only in two colors, gray and black.

Plate 117.

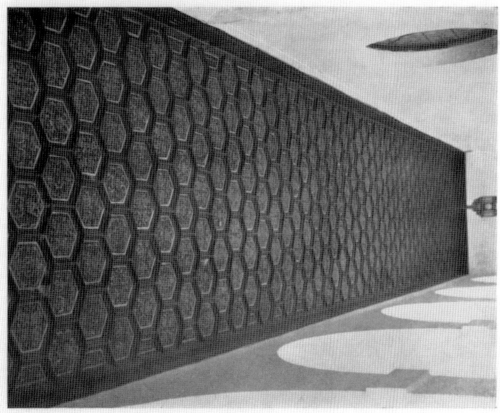

A Beamed Ceiling in Seville.

The ceiling here shown is in a modern residence near the Plaza de San Fernando. It is built in a manner much favored in Seville, i. e., three series of intersecting beams varying in depth according to their importance as structural members.

The ceiling is thus divided into small rectangles, and the effect is sufficiently interesting to require little enrichment with moldings, carvings or color.

Old Ceiling in Monastery near Segovia.

In the ruins of the Monastery of Parral, across the Erasma from Segovia, is this simple but interesting old wooden ceiling in what probably was once the refectory. The decorations, done in dull colors, must have been very effective before they were effaced by later coats of whitewash.

Plate 118.

A Coffered Ceiling in Valencia.

This is one of the two elaborate Renaissance ceilings in the 16th century building known as the Audiencia. It is in the Salon de Cortes, and is surrounded by a narrow arcaded gallery lavishly ornamented in the bold and unrestricted manner characteristic of the Spaniards. The deep ceiling coffers are richly carved red cedar left in the natural finish of the wood. There is a long carved pendant in each of the center diamonds, and smaller ones in each of the triangular corners.

Detail of Ceiling in Toledo.

This is a perpendicular view of the fine old coffered ceiling shown on plate 117. The Spanish treatment of their coffered ceilings, leaving them in the natural wood without color decoration, is remarkably rich and handsome. There is no feeling of garishness, even when lavishly ornamented as in the ceiling above.

Plate 119.

Fireplace in Toledo.

In a large upper room of a fine old Moorish palace in Toledo, now owned by the Conde de Toledo, is this elaborate and unusual Gothic fireplace. It is one of the many curious accessions to this interesting old relic of the Moors, made by the Spaniards during the centuries since the conquest.

Fireplace in Seville.

Although more elaborate and finished than those usually found in Spanish homes, this fireplace contains their typical features and accessories. It is in the tower room on the second floor of the famous palace now belonging to the Duke of Alba, of which the ceiling was shown on plate 115.

Plate 120.

SECTION K
FOUNTAINS, FLOORS, WALLS AND GATES

FOUNTAINS, FLOORS, WALLS AND GATES

AN essential feature of Moorish gardens was water; used not with gushing, blatant effect as in Italian fountains and cascades, but in the modest manner of tiny jets falling into small receptacles. From these it rippled through open channels along pathways and down stairways to other basins or to water effects below. Sometimes it emptied into great quiet pools in which the mirrored images of surrounding buildings and landscape added depth and mystery to the enchanting scene. The presence of water pervaded not only the luxuriant gardens but the principal rooms of the residence or palace to which they were joined. The refreshing coolness and soft musical cadence of gently spraying and flowing water was a relaxing and lulling influence conducive to meditation and repose.

The Spaniard, with his many oriental characteristics, was imbued with the delectable charm of Moorish gardens and has, since the conquest, adopted their distinctive features for his own. The Spanish gardens are bright and gay, yet they are quiet and restful due to the pleasing harmony of their elements. Every detail and accessory adds an unobtrusive note of color and interest. Even the walks and pavements are laid out in delightful patterns, sometimes with only the slight color variation of beach pebbles but more often with the brilliant hues of decorated tile. The Spaniard loves seclusion in his domestic life and, therefore, it is a requisite in his patios and gardens. When the building does not entirely surround the patio, or when the gardens extend beyond the confines of the house, high masonry walls enclose the otherwise exposed borders of the gardens. These walls are usually massive and severe, unadorned except for a simple tile coping used as a protection from the elements. The interior wall faces are screened with vines, high growing shrubs or pleached hedges of trees. An interesting feature of these protecting walls are the gateways which are sometimes provided for access from the outside, or for communication between gardens where walls separate the plots. In palace gardens or those of a public nature, the gateways are sometimes ornamented in the elaborate manner of the doorways to the buildings; but usually they are as simple and free from ostentation as the walls, giving little evidence of the luxuriance and beauty of the scenes they seclude.

Pool in Old Andalusian Patio.

In a corner of many old patios in southern Spain, a trough was provided for watering the horses and other stock kept in stalls adjoining the patio. Where the trough is no longer used for this purpose, it has been converted into a pool for aquatic plants and goldfishes. The broad, flat top of the enclosing curb is used for the display of potted plants.

Plate 121.

A Small Garden Fountain in Granada.

In the tea garden recently added to the Washington Irving Hotel in Granada, is this delightful little fountain.

The shallow, octagonal pool, bordered with blue and white tile, is only slightly raised above the floor of the garden, and is filled with potted plants. From the center rises a fine jet of water. It is unpretentious features, such as these, that give Spanish gardens their enduring charm.

An unusual Garden Feature in Malaga.

This is a quaint conceit, combining a fountain and sundial made of polychrome tile. It is one of the many interesting features of the beautiful city park in Malaga. This extensive park is a splendid demonstration of logical city beautification. It is a waterfront improvement on land reclaimed from dredging the harbor and greatly enhances the attractiveness of the city.

Plate 122.

Fountains in the Alcazar Gardens, Seville.

The gardens adjoining the famous Alcazar in Seville are among the largest and best known in Spain. They are of Moorish origin but have been greatly altered and reconstructed since the palace became the home of Spanish sovereigns. However, the gardens still contain many of the delightful Moorish features: potted plants massed in the patios and decorating the walls; colored tile seats, pavements and accessories; and simple water effects, pools, rivulets and fountains. The musical ripple and gurgle of water can be heard throughout the gardens.

Plate 123.

Fountains in the Alcazar Gardens,—Continued.

At every path intersection in the garden is a fountain. Every fountain is of a different form and treatment.

The tops of the pools are set flush with the pavement and are shaped in interesting geometrical patterns. Some of the pools overflow the curbs onto the colored tile pavement, and drop into a surrounding gutter from whence the water is conveyed through the gardens in open channels, usually down the center of the paths and stairways.

Plate 124.

Fountains in the Alcazar Gardens,—Continued.

Many and varied are the fountain designs. Sometimes the jets spring from small basins set in the pavement, but usually the bowls are raised above pools, supported on ornamental pedestals. Instead of overflowing their rims, the bowls are provided with a series of spouts through which the water drops in streams to the pool below. The streams are regulated and kept uniform by valves in the spouts.

Plate 125.

Vistas in the Alcazar Gardens, Seville.

The most noteworthy feature in the plan of the Alcazar gardens is the location of the fountains at the path intersections throughout the gardens. They greatly enhance the beauty of the long vistas through the dense growth that embowers the pathways. At each fountain the open space is enlarged to accommodate bright tiled seats or garden benches which are placed at the borders, against the background of foliage. Note in the lower view, how the bottom of the water channel, down the stairway, is roughened to produce rippling effects as the water courses from one fountain to the next one below.

Plate 126.

FOUNTAINS, FLOORS, WALLS AND GATES

Pebbled Pavement in a Patio, Cordova.

In the Alhambra gardens and many of the Moorish designed patios of southern Spain, are to be seen unusual walks and pavements made of small, worn pebbles of various shades, worked into graceful and interesting designs. This pebble work is particularly delightful when used in combination with colored tile, either as a narrow raised curb, as here shown, or as a broad border flanking the walks, and upon which potted plants are ranged.

A Decorated Patio Floor in Seville.

Patterned floors of decorated colored tile are a typical patio treatment in Andalusia. They form a pleasing background and base for the deep green foliage of the potted plants. The effect is often as rich and harmonious as the design and colorings of fine old oriental rugs.

Plate 127.

An Italian Treatment of a Garden Wall.

This is a quiet nook in the spectacular gardens of the Villa d'Este near Tivoli. The custom of combining seats with walls in Mediterranean gardens is interestingly exemplified in this view. The open, tile construction of the parapets above the seats serves effectively as a screen, yet permits glimpses through into the gardens below.

A Garden Wall in Granada.

Less architectural, but no less interesting is the treatment of combination walls and seats in the unpretentious gardens of Spain. Colored tile and potted plants are less obtrusive and in better harmony than ornate embellishments.

Plate 128.

Plate 129.

A Garden Wall in Algeciras, Spain.

A very practical and satisfying treatment of a garden wall built down a steep hillside, is shown in this picture. The masonry was extended high enough to give privacy from the street; and the open iron railing between the posts above protects from intrusion but does not shut out the view from the terraced gardens within.

Plate 129.

A Garden Wall in Algiers.

This is an unusually effective treatment of a wall built as a screen at the end of a garden terrace. The tiled plant shelf lines with the top of the front parapet of the terrace.

Note the decorative effect of the tree branch extending through a breach left in the wall for the purpose.

A Novel Wall Treatment in Gibraltar.

This crude masonry wall is relieved of severity by building in flower pots on the plain top of the wall.

Plate 130.

A Garden Wall in Rabat, Morocco.

This modern wall enclosing the grounds of a government building, shows an unusual design of concrete wall and post construction, filled in between the posts with wooden railing.

The concrete is finished with stucco excepting the circles of ornamentation near the top of the posts. These ornaments are made by chiseling the concrete to produce the star design.

A Garden Balustrade in Algiers.

Another novel design for a modern garden feature is the balustrade here shown. The heavy posts are projections from the concrete retaining wall of an elevated terrace in a spacious hotel garden above the old city of Algiers.

The openwork parapet is also of cast concrete.

Plate 131.

Old Garden Walls and Gateways in Spain.

These are examples of the thick, crude old walls which surround many of the gardens, and enclose many of the country places in Spain. In the old work, the walls of the gardens and also the buildings were rudely constructed of rock rubble, and given a semblance of finish with white-washed stucco.

Plate 132.

SECTION L
ORNAMENTAL IRON WORK

ORNAMENTAL IRON WORK

IRON has occupied a place of great importance since the Middle Ages as a metal particularly suited for decorative work. During the Renaissance, malleable iron was extensively used throughout Europe to enrich and beautify such practical features of the buildings as balconies, grilles, railings, screens and gates. It was fashioned into lamp standards, lanterns, hardware, and embellishments for doors, shutters and furniture. Wrought iron is peculiarly adaptable for this work because of its comparative cheapness, hardness, strength and malleability; and particularly on account of the facility with which it can be forged and welded, properties which are possessed only by iron. A serious inherent defect is its rapid deterioration by rusting unless its surface is protected by a preservative coating. While the old process of treating iron to protect it from rusting is one of the lost arts, it is believed that the means employed was to plunge the heated metal into an oil which would penetrate the surface sufficiently to minimize oxidation.

While England, France and Italy furnish many fine examples of Medieval iron work, it is in Spain that we find the finest expressions of the art. There, the Moors, with their superior craftsmanship and innate cleverness as ornamentalists, profoundly influenced the development of architecture, and particularly the decoration of construction details. Geometrical forms were the basis of decorative motifs employed by the Moors, and their designs were well suited to the qualities and peculiarities of wrought iron. Their fine comprehension of the fundamental principle of architectural decoration,—ornamenting construction, and not merely constructing and applying ornament,—and also their frank disregard for conventional forms and styles unless they particularly suited their ideas and purposes, strongly appealed to the Spanish character. As wrought iron possesses the qualities most desired,—strength and ductility—which make it so adaptable for decorative construction, it is not surprising that, in a short time after its introduction, ornamental iron work became a characteristic of Spanish architecture. There is hardly a building of pretension in which iron work is not proudly featured. Almost every window has its ornamental iron grille or balcony; and doors in Spain have been glorified with hinge straps, bosses, knockers and escutcheons developed to a point of grace and beauty undreamed of elsewhere.

ORNAMENTAL IRON WORK

Knocker on Cathedral Door, Tarragona, Spain.

Some of the finest examples of iron craftsmanship in Spain are the knockers used so generally on the entrance doors to residences as well as to public buildings. The specimen here shown is the feature of the great metal-covered doors of the main portal in the fine old 14th century cathedral in Tarragona. This knocker has quite the richness and delicacy of silver work. Much of the best architectural decoration in Spain was designed in the spirit of the silversmith's work, and the style is known as the "Plateresque."

Knocker on Door to Public Building,
Ragusa, Jugo-Slavia.

Knockers were a popular door embellishment during the centuries of the Renaissance. They were usually made of iron or bronze, and many and varied were the interesting designs used.

Plate 133.

Detail of Iron Studded Door in Seville.

A favorite method of the Moors for enriching a door was with decorative nail heads, bosses, or thin pieces of metal cut to pattern and fastened with nails through the center. These were placed in rows or simple designs on the plain plank surface of the doors. This treatment was introduced into Spain by the Moors, and is an Oriental development peculiar to that country.

A Door Knocker in Barcelona.

A fine example of forged iron work in which the art and skill of the Spaniard is well displayed. It is excellent, not only in design but in execution. No attempt was made to conceal the fact that it is of wrought iron. The slight irregularity of the ring and the crudity of finish evidences the metal and the process by which the work was done.

Plate 134.

ORNAMENTAL IRON WORK

Plate 135.

Ornamental Hardware on Doors in Spain.

The Spaniards have been adepts in every form and treatment of ornamental iron work, from the rough forging of structural members to the delicate cutting and incising of escutcheons and cabinet hardware. While it may be said that the Spaniards possess little originality, they have displayed great ingenuity in adapting and combining decorative styles to suit their peculiar tastes and expediencies.

Plate 135.

Ornamental Iron Railings in Spain.

The simple types of iron railings peculiar to Spain have been illustrated in previous sections showing grilles, balconies and stairways. Seldom have the intricacies of the Moorish Arabesque, or the floridities of the French Baroque influenced the design of iron work in Spain. Here, however, are illustrated two interesting exceptions. The upper picture is of a railing in the Alcazar in Seville; the lower shows a section of an elaborate stair-railing in an 18th century palace in Palma, Mallorca.

Plate 136.

An Old Well Head in Granada.

Many excellent examples of wrought iron well heads are to be found in the patios of Spain, and also in the cloister gardens of its churches and monasteries. The one here shown is a particularly fine specimen of Spanish forged work.

It no longer serves as a superstructure for a well, but is used merely as a decorative note in an old patio in Granada.

Plate 137.

An Old Well Head in Toledo.

This is another interesting relic of old Spain found in the Moorish house of del Conde de Toledo. Stone well curbs are more common in Spain than those of wrought iron. The pot holders supported on the standards of the pulley frame are a delightful innovation.

Plate 138.

Two More Spanish Well Heads.

Like many other practical features of Spanish buildings and gardens, the well head with its curb and pulley structure, has been made a thing of interest and beauty.

The upper scene is in the stable yard of a fine old country palace on the Island of Mallorca.

The well shown in the lower picture is unusually located on a flat-roofed upper story section of the Alcazar in Segovia.

Plate 139.

An Unusual Light Standard in Village Between
Seville and Huelva.

Among the miscellaneous objects made of wrought
iron, frequently seen in Spain, are weather vanes, finials
and crosses, often of fantastic design. They are generally
used to crown the towers and domes of buildings, both
religious and secular, and their dark silhouettes against
the sky add much to the picturesque charm of the compositions.

Iron crosses are sometimes seen along the wayside as
boundary markers, or surmounting a column in the open
squares, or plazas, of the towns. Often they are of novel
design and serve as light standards, as here shown.

Plate 140.

Plate 141.

Gate to Public Market in Ronda.

A characteristic feature of the design of grilles, gates and railings in Andalusian towns is a continuous pattern formed of simple scrolls effectively used in repetition, as shown in this picture.

Plate 141.

Entrance Door Grilles in Seville.

The doorway of Sevillian houses gives direct entrance to the patio. They are generous openings filled in with iron grille work, often elaborately intricate in design, particularly in recent work.

The upper picture shows a typical entrance to a modern home in Seville.

The lower view is of a garden entrance in the Alcazar. It is of wrought iron in the characteristic Arabesque style of the Moors.

Plate 142.

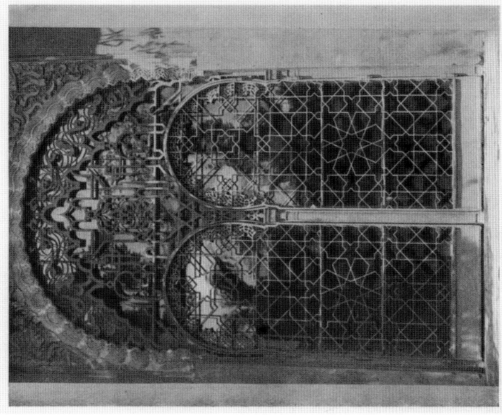

Round, Grilled Windows in Buildings, Seville.

While not commonly used, round windows are occasionally seen in Spain. A circular opening not only gives interest to an otherwise severe facade, but also an opportunity to display a delightful bit of wrought iron design. Round openings, covered with grille, sometimes serve as gable-end vents to roof spaces.

Plate 143.

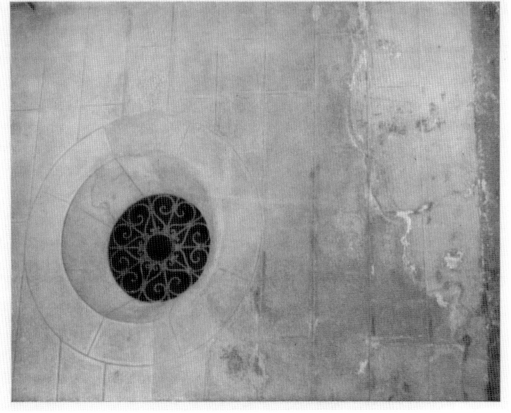

Examples of Lighting Fixtures in Spain.

Another interesting and practical use of wrought iron in Spain is shown in the bracket lanterns which frequently adorn and illuminate the arcades, loggias, patios and gardens.

The lanterns shown in the two upper pictures are garden features in Ronda, they are made entirely of wrought iron.

The two lower views were taken in patio arcades, (left) in Seville, and (right) in Toledo. The metal work of the lanterns is brass, and they are executed in the Oriental style suggestive of Turkey.

Plate 144.